Cooking Fun with Mrs. Cubbage

ACKNOWLEDGEMENTS

Thank you to the parents who trust/trusted me to teach their children about cooking.

Thank you to the community center for giving me the chance, and seeing something in me.

To my husband, Samuel Cubbage, for listening to me complain about wanting to 'get this book published!!!' LOL!! I love you!

And of course, the children. I have enjoyed having you in my class; cooking, cleaning up, taste- testing, telling stories and you telling me your stories. AND coming up with some of our own stories and memories!

INTRODUCTION

One of the things I LOVE to do is teach the children! They bring an energy and a sense of joy to EVERY subject they are interested in. One thing that I've found is that if you are a teacher who walks into a room of children, with some form of FOOD in your arms….(lol!), you INSTANTLY become the "fan favorite"!

Several years ago, the community center in my neighborhood had a wonderful teacher, who did cooking classes, with small children. (Ages 5-9)

Since I had the background, working WITH small children, and this teacher was retiring, I was approached about taking her place.

I had never really COOKED with young children before; and knew that IF I were going to TEACH children about cooking, that I had to LEARN first; LEARN about what they could do. What they actually knew and understood about cooking; AND IF they were capable of doing this complicated, multi-stepped activity.

I am pleased to say that the children that I've come in contact with, have MORE that exceeded my expectations! You must KNOW your audience, and KNOW what they want and what they can achieve. And not only that; that you do not give them a task too difficult, that they become discouraged.

Many of these children have had the opportunity to cook in the kitchen with their own families; but, many of them have not. So, I was blessed to be their very first cooking experience!

Children are very interested in learning something 'hands-on'. If they can get their hands into some dough, cake mix, cut something, etc., they are truly, "happy campers"!

Since becoming a teacher, I have had the opportunity to do several cooking classes with lots of different children.

In this cookbook, I've tried to create a menu of foods that are easy to learn, tasty to eat, and that the children could get some type of memorable lesson from it. But, I must say, once we got started, I was the one who was getting the lesson… HAHA!

Here is a collection of recipes that I have performed WITH the children, IN the classroom! ALL of these recipes were done WITHOUT an oven! Truly...

I hope that you not only ENJOY the stories and recipes; but, ENJOY these recipes with your own children.

DEDICATION

This book is dedicated to each and every child that took any of my cooking classes. Thank you for making me THINK about cooking at YOUR level. And THANK YOU for making this possible.

TABLE OF CONTENTS

Lunch

1. Turkey roll up

Desserts

1. Doughnut Holes
2. Trash can popcorn
3. Rice Crispy bites on a stick

APPETIZERS

Over the years, one thing I learned is that the children are NOT interested in ACTUALLY learning about what each kitchen utensil can do; they are ready to get Messy, and EAT! This particular recipe is SOOOO easy! But, if you do not assign enough jobs for/to the children, you are going to have a lot of little people asking, "What's next? What can I do? Can I do what he's doing?" So, break up the instructions and ingredients into as many children that you have. That will slow down (not stop) the many questions that are sure to come your way.

Easy, Homemade Salsa

Ingredients

- Fresh tomatoes – use the nice, red ones, avoid anything soft.
- Fresh cilantro – cilantro adds the nice flavor.
- Yellow onion- green onion can be used here, as well.
- Garlic
- Lime – gives the salsa a boost! .
- Chili powder
- Sugar – just a pinch. It helps to balance the acidity of the tomatoes and lime.
- Salt and pepper – to taste

Directions

Chop ALL of the vegetables, and put them into a large bowl. Combine garlic, onion, 1/2 teaspoon salt, and 1/4 teaspoon pepper. Add the tomatoes, lime juice, and oil and toss to combine. Fold in the cilantro.
Put in the refrigerator for 30 minutes. Grab your favorite bag of tortilla chips! Enjoy!

Spanakopita

Ingredients

- 3 tablespoons olive oil
- 1 large onion, chopped
- 2 cloves garlic, minced
- 2 pounds spinach, rinsed and chopped
- 1/2 cup chopped fresh parsley (Preferred)
- 2 eggs, lightly beaten
- 1/2 cup ricotta cheese
- 1 cup crumbled feta cheese
- 8 sheets phyllo dough

Directions

1. Preheat the oven to 350 degrees F. Lightly oil a 9x9 inch square baking pan.

2. Heat 3 tablespoons olive oil in a large skillet over medium heat. Saute onion, green onions and garlic, until soft and golden brown. Stir in spinach and parsley, and continue to saute until spinach is soft, about 2 minutes. Remove from heat and set aside.

3. In a medium bowl, mix together eggs, ricotta, and feta. Stir in spinach mixture. Lay 1 sheet of phyllo dough in a prepared baking pan, and brush lightly with olive oil. Lay another sheet of phyllo dough on top, brush with olive oil, and repeat the process with two more sheets of phyllo. The sheets will overlap the pan. Spread spinach and cheese mixture into pan and fold overhanging dough over filling. Brush with oil, then layer remaining 4 sheets of phyllo dough, brushing each with oil. Tuck in the overhanging dough into the pan to seal the filling.

4. Bake in a preheated oven for 35 minutes. Or, until golden brown. Cut into squares; usually you would serve it hot. But, with the children, wait for a little while, and then serve.

Side Dishes

Macaroni and cheese! ALWAYS a fan favorite! Now, some of the ingredients the children may not like (because they are used to the powdered mac and cheese). But, once they give it a try, they gobble it up!

Macaroni and cheese

INGREDIENTS

- 1 pound elbow noodles
- 1/2 cup salted butter
- 1/2 cup all-purpose flour
- 1/2 teaspoon onion powder
- 1/2 teaspoon garlic powder
- 1 teaspoon salt
- 1/2 teaspoon pepper
- 3 cups milk whole, 2%, or 1%
- 8 ounces shredded sharp cheddar cheese

INSTRUCTIONS

1. Fill a large saucepan with water, and bring to a boil. Stir in the macaroni; cook until al dente. Drain well.

2. In another large saucepan, melt the butter over medium heat. Stir in the flour, salt, pepper, onion powder, and garlic powder and cook 1-2 minutes.

3. Pour in milk and whisk until smooth. Cook over medium-high heat, stirring constantly, for 3-5 minutes until the sauce starts to thicken. Turn off the heat and whisk in cheese until melted.

4. Pour cooked pasta into the cheese sauce and stir well to combine. Serve warm.

Easy Skillet Stuffing

Ingredients

2 small onions diced
4 stalks celery diced
⅔ cup butter
½ teaspoons ground sage
black pepper and salt to taste
12 cups bread cubes
3-4 cups chicken broth
2 tablespoons fresh parsley
1 tablespoon fresh herbs (*Sage and Rosemary*

Instructions

1. Melt butter in a large skillet over medium heat. Add onion, celery and poultry seasoning (and rosemary). Cook over medium-low until tender (do not brown), about 10-12 minutes.
2. Place bread cubes in a large bowl. Add onion mixture, parsley and fresh herbs.
3. Pour broth overtop until cubes are moist (but not wet and soggy) gently mix. You may not need all of the broth. Season with salt and pepper to taste.
4. Keep in the skillet on low heat, for 7 more minutes. Serve warm.

FRESH SALADS

A fresh garden salad…. Mmmmmm! Doesn't that sound good! Well, the children don't always think so…lol! However, they REALLY enjoy the chopping, slicing and dicing! One of the easiest of recipes, a fresh garden salad is a GREAT start to teaching the children how to operate kitchen utensils.

Fresh Garden Salad

Ingredients:
1 Head of Lettuce
3 Tomatoes
2 Carrots
3 Cucumbers
Your child's favorite salad dressing

Directions:
Make sure to wash all vegetables before use.
On a cutting board, cut all of the vegetables, into small bite sized pieces, adding to a large salad bowl.
Add the salad dressing. And serve!

For this recipe, you need to look at the "Fresh garden salad" recipe, then add chicken breast! That's all! Very yummy! And VERY simple! Your child will enjoy this one...largely because of the chicken! HAHA!

Fresh Chicken Salad

Refer to the "Fresh garden salad" recipe on the previous page.

How to prepare the chicken.

- Heat ¼ tablespoon of oil or canola oil in a large skillet.

- Season the chicken breasts on both sides with salt, ground pepper, garlic powder and dried basil. When oil is hot, add chicken breasts to the pan – cook two chicken breasts at a time because you don't want to overcrowd your skillet.

- Cook chicken breasts for 7 to 10 minutes. Flip the chicken breasts over, add a tablespoon of butter to the skillet, and continue to cook for 7 more minutes, or until internal temperature reaches 165F. Cooking time will always depend on the thickness of the chicken breasts. When finished, transfer chicken breasts to a cutting board; let rest for 5 minutes, then slice and add to the salad and serve!

WARM AND TASTY SOUPS!

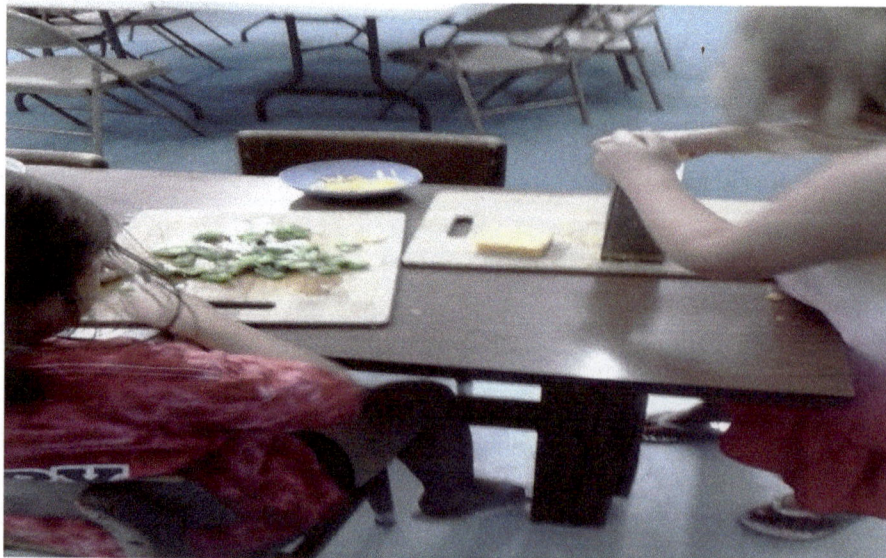

I'm not going to lie. Kids do NOT like tomato soup... well, let me rephrase that! They like CANNED tomato soup. Not MAKING tomato soup! So, they WILL enjoy the MAKING and PREPARATION of this activity. However, unless your child likes tomatoes, or soup, this may NOT be the best recipe. (Another mistake that I made was that I used FRESH tomatoes, too! In hindsight, I probably should have used canned tomatoes. So, this recipe will have the canned tomatoes---but, will include the fresh tomatoes...if you so choose!

Homemade tomato soup

Ingredients

4 tablespoons unsalted butter

1/2 large onion, cut into large wedges

1 (28-ounce) can tomatoes, whole peeled or crushed, see notes for fresh tomatoes. Can I use fresh tomatoes? Yes. If you want to use fresh tomatoes, you will need 9-10 medium tomatoes (about 2 pounds). You can peel them, but you can skip this part if you are using a blender.

1 1/2 cups water, low sodium vegetable or chicken stock

1/2 teaspoon fine sea salt and basil, or more to taste

Directions

Melt butter over medium heat in a large saucepan.

Add onion wedges, water, can of tomatoes with their juices, and 1/2 teaspoon of salt. Bring to a simmer. Cook, uncovered, for about 40 minutes. Stirring occasionally.

Blend the soup, and then season to taste. The soup doesn't need to be super smooth. Use a blender. If you use a regular blender, blend the soup in stages and do not fill the blender as much as you normally would since the soup is hot. Once the soup is blended to your liking, feel free to enjoy!

Homemade Potato soup

Ingredients

- 6 bacon strips, diced
- 6 large potatoes (cubed)
- 1 small carrot, grated
- 1/2 cup chopped onion
- 1 can (14-1/2 ounces) chicken broth
- 3 tablespoons all-purpose flour
- 3 cups milk (feel free to use whatever type of milk you like. For the children, I found that 1% milk worked well)
- 8 ounces sharp cheddar cheese

Directions

Peel the potatoes with a potato peeler. Then, boil a half pot of water. Place potatoes in the water and boil for about 20 minutes. While the potatoes are boiling, you can start on the other steps.

- In a large saucepan, cook bacon over medium heat until crisp, stirring occasionally; drain drippings. Then, use the drippings to saute the onions
- Add vegetables, including potatoes, seasonings and broth; bring to a boil. Reduce heat; simmer, covered, until potatoes are tender, 10-15 minutes.
- Mix flour and milk until smooth; stir into soup. Bring to a boil, stirring constantly; cook and stir until thickened, about 2 minutes. Stir in cheese until melted. Add a dollop of sour cream, crumble your bacon and enjoy!

Breakfast time! Rise and Shine!

Egg in a Hole

Ingredients:

  1 Pat of butter
1 slice of your favorite bread
1 egg
Salt and pepper to taste

Directions:

Melt the butter in a skillet

With the top of a small water glass, cut a hole from the center of the bread slice; lay in the hot skillet. When the side facing down is lightly toasted, about 1-2 minutes, flip and crack the egg into the hole; season with salt and pepper. Continue to cook until the egg is cooked and somewhat firm. Flip over and cook 1 minute more to make sure that it is done on both sides. Serve right away.

MAIN DISHES

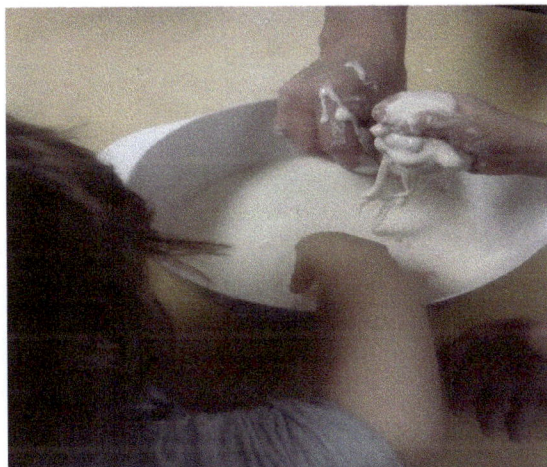

Skillet Pizza

1 pound pizza dough, at room temperature 1 hour

1 to 2 teaspoons vegetable or olive oil

1 cup pizza sauce

2 cups shredded provolone and mozzarella cheese

1 to 2 cups toppings, cooked sausage, pepperoni- or any other favorite toppings

Instructions

1. **Prepare the toppings.** Have the sauce, shredded cheese, and other toppings ready to go. Cook any raw toppings that you want cooked before assembling the pizza. Arrange all of the toppings within easy reach of the stove, where you'll be cooking the pizza.

2. **Roll out the pizza dough.** Divide the dough in half. Lightly flour your counter and then press or roll one piece of the dough into a round that's slightly smaller than the skillet you will be using -- you will need a 10 or 12-inch cast iron, stainless steel, or nonstick skillet.

3. **Heat the skillet.** Place the skillet over medium-high heat and add a teaspoon or two of the oil. You want just enough oil to slick the bottom of the pan. Heat until the oil is shimmering.

4. **Cook the pizza for 1 minute.** Transfer the round of pizza dough to the pan. Cook until you see large bubbles forming on top and the underside shows golden spots, about 1 minute. You can deflate the bubbles with the edge of your spatula — or leave them! They'll turn into crispy bits once you flip the pizza.

5. **Flip the crust and add toppings.** Use a flat spatula to flip the pizza dough. Immediately top with a few spoonfuls of sauce, a generous sprinkle of cheese, and other toppings.

6. **Cover and reduce the heat to medium.** Cover the skillet and reduce the heat to medium. This helps the cheese melt and prevents the bottom of the pizza from burning.

7. **Cook the pizza for another 4 to 5 minutes.** After 4 minutes, peek under the lid and see if the cheese has melted. Cover and continue cooking if needed; adjust the heat as

needed to make sure the bottom gets golden-brown but doesn't burn. The pizza is ready as soon as the cheese has melted to your liking.

The favorite of ALL favorites! Kids LOVE cheese! And this will definitely get their attention!

Grilled cheese

INGREDIENTS

5 tbsp. butter, softened, divided

4 slices of your favorite bread

2 c. shredded or slices of your favorite cheese

DIRECTIONS

Spread 1 tablespoon butter on one side of each slice of bread. With butter side down, top each slice of bread with about ½ cup cheese. In a skillet over medium heat, melt 1 tablespoon butter. Add two slices of bread, butter side down. Cook until bread is toasty, golden brown and cheese has started to melt; about 2.5 minutes. Flip one piece of bread on top of the other and continue to cook until the cheese has melted. Enjoy!

Lunch!

Turkey roll up

Ingredients

½ cup mayonnaise or salad dressing

4 oz cream cheese, softened

2 tablespoons chopped fresh cilantro

4 slices bacon, crisply cooked, crumbled

6 flour tortillas, 8-inch (from 11.5-oz package)

½ lb thinly sliced cooked turkey

Directions

In a small bowl, mix mayonnaise and cream cheese until smooth. Stir in cilantro and bacon. Warm tortillas as directed on the package. Spread about 2 tablespoons mayonnaise mixture on each tortilla. Top each with 1 slice of turkey. Roll up each tortilla tightly. Cut each roll into 8 pieces. (Sometimes my students don't want it cut. In that case... Eat!

Desserts

Doughnut/ Donut holes! This was a HUGE hit! So much so, that when I taught this lesson, one of my students brought me some donut holes that SHE made with her mom!

Doughnut Holes

Ingredients

Vegetable oil or canola oil for frying

2 cups all-purpose flour

3 Tbsp sugar

1 Tbsp baking powder

1 tsp salt

5 Tbsp butter cold

3/4 cups milk

For rolling

1/3 cup granulated sugar

1 1/2 tsp ground cinnamon

Instructions

Combine flour, sugar, baking powder and salt and mix. Using a pastry cutter, cut butter into your flour mixture, until it becomes crumbly. Add milk and mix until all ingredients are combined. Put the dough onto a well-floured, flat surface, and knead gently until it forms a smooth ball. If dough is too sticky to manage, continue to use the flour until it is smooth and workable. Pull off about 1 ½ inch sized pieces of dough, and roll into smooth, tight balls. Set aside.

Fill a medium-sized saucepan with about 2 inches of oil, over medium-high heat. You will have to monitor the heat regularly; and may need to increase or decrease your stovetop temperature.

While your oil is heating, prepare your cinnamon/sugar mix by stirring together cinnamon and sugar in a small dish. Set aside.

Have a plate ready for your cooked donut holes, covered in paper towels.

Once oil is heated and ready, carefully fry your donut holes, about 6 at a time, carefully placing them into the oil with a slotted spoon (don't drop them in or the oil may splash, lower them into the oil instead. An older child can help with this. Not the toddlers).

Fry donut holes for 3 minutes, remove carefully with a slotted spoon, and place them on the paper towel plate. Allow them to sit for about 30 seconds and then use another spoon to transfer them to your cinnamon/sugar dish. Roll them in the topping until fully covered. Have another plate available for the finished product. (We have also used powdered sugar for a topping.) They are best on that same day. However, you can get away with having them the next day.

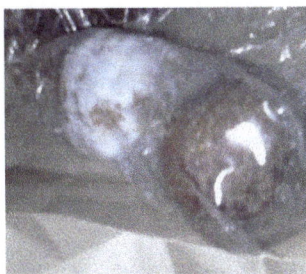

TRASH CAN POPCORN

Ingredients:

Popcorn

Cookies

Candy (any kind that you have)

Directions:

Mix all ingredients together! The kids will love it! Then, melt chocolate all over the popcorn! Let the chocolate cool.... Then, One... two... three... EAT!

Rice Crispy bites on a stick

Ingredients:
6 tablespoons of salted butter
16 ounces of Marshmallows
7 cups of Rice Krispies Cereal
3 cups of your favorite chocolate

Directions:
Melt 6 tablespoons of Salted Butter with 16 ounces marshmallows. Stir in 7 cups of Rice Krispies Cereal and gently pat into a well-buttered 9 X 13-inch pan. Allow the treats to cool completely. In a small pot, melt your favorite chocolate. You can use pure dark, semi-sweet, milk chocolate or white chocolate. Cut the Rice Krispies treats into 1 inch squares, and add it to a confection stick. Carefully dip each stick of Rice Krispies treats, into the melted chocolate. On a flat surface, have a sheet of wax paper ready. Place each treat on the wax paper. Allow treats to cool. Then, Enjoy!